# God, Why Does It Feel Like You Do Not Exist

*I am Dawn:*
*A Cry for Meaning*
*in a World That's Breaking*

Sahar Soltani

**Copyright © 2025 by Sahar Soltani**
*All rights reserved.*
No part of this book may be reproduced or transmitted in any form or by any means, electronic, mechanical, photocopying, recording, or otherwise, without prior written permission from the author, except in the case of brief quotations used in articles, reviews, or academic references.

This book is a work of personal nonfiction, drawn from the author's own journals, reflections, and spiritual journey. All writings represent the author's lived experience, sincere study and prayerful wrestling with YHWH. Readers are encouraged to seek the Scriptures and the Spirit of YHWH for their own discernment and understanding. While the experiences and insights are authentically the author's, they are not presented as doctrine but as witness to brokenness, searching, and the fire that comes from encountering Him.

This work is independently written, self-published, and self-imposed, and is not affiliated with any religious denomination, institution, or publishing house. All Scripture quotations in this work are rendered in restored form, referencing the original Hebrew, Aramaic and Greek texts as closely as possible, with Divine Names such as **YHWH** and **Yeshua** restored where they were obscured in mainstream translations.

Published by The Quiet Seer Press
For inquiries: quietseerpress@outlook.com
Cover and interior design by Sahar Soltani
ISBN: 978-1-0698031-1-5

To those who have always lived in pain.

To those who have always wondered
why their suffering never ends.

To those who mock Him
and blame Him
for all the pain in this world.

To those who have ever asked
if He even exists.

To those who believe
that chaos and pain
must mean the absence of God.

To those who have wanted
to release their last weary breath,
not knowing that life
was always meant to be eternal.

To those who have cried
and battled,
and lived through the fire,
never realizing
it was never their strength
that carried them,

but One alone.

To those who thought
their strength was enough.
To those who trusted
their knowledge.
To those who believed
their human capacity
could save them.

To those who tried
to control the uncontrollable.

To those who thought
they could predict their own future
and let it unfold
through temporary eyes.

To those who believed
nothing could protect them
but their own willpower or wealth.

To those who refused to surrender
to the only One who shields from darkness,
even the unspeakable Abyss.

To those who could not lay down their pride,

their intellect,
their need to be right,

and because of it,
risked losing everything
when they could have gained everything.

To those who still have breath,
this is for you.

Because every breath you've drawn,
every sigh, every cry,
was a whisper of His Name.
It was His to begin with,
all along.

*Aleph (א) is the first letter of the Hebrew alphabet.*
*It carries no sound like breath.*
*It is the beginning of "Elohim" and "I AM."*

Say it: **YHWH** — *Breath.*

The ***I AM*** you've been breathing all along.

---

"YHWH" (יהוה) is the sacred Name revealed to Moses in Exodus 3:14, often rendered "I AM." In Hebrew, it is composed of the breath sounds Yod–Hey–Vav–Hey, making it literally unspeakable—like breathing itself. This is why many say the name of God is the sound of breath: the I AM you've been breathing all along.

## Author's Note

This book was not written in comfort.
It was born in the pit,
in the silence where I begged God to show me
He was still there.

Where I asked why the screams of suffering
seemed louder than mercy.
Where I wept over a world that feels like it's
breaking apart.

But through the ache, something happened.
Not a tidy answer.
Not an escape.
But a Presence.

Yeshua.
Not the version religion offers.
Not the cultural icon.
But the I AM Himself.

He met me there.
In the quiet.
In the fire.

And through it,
I began to see that He was never distant,
only veiled by pain I hadn't yet understood.
Pain that was necessary to close
my temporary eyes,
and open the ones
made for eternity.

This book is not a theology textbook.
It is a cry.
A scroll.
A revelation.

For those who feel too sensitive.
Too confused.
Too heartbroken to keep pretending.

It is for the hidden ones.
The almost-gave-ups.
The exiles.
The ones who still whisper prayers,
even when they don't know if anyone is
listening.

To the ones left behind.
To the remnant yet to come.

I didn't write this to convince you.
I wrote it because I couldn't stay silent anymore.

And if something in these pages
echoes inside you,
if it stirs even a flicker of hope or truth,
then perhaps laying my soul bare
in all its rawness and ache
was worth it.

And if that wasn't enough,
then maybe every scar it took to birth this
was.

I am Sahar.
And I rise not to be seen,
but to say:

*Tav (ת) is the last letter of the Hebrew alphabet.*
*In ancient Paleo-Hebrew, its shape was the cross*
*foreshadowing the sign of the covenant.*
*Even in the letters, YHWH was always revealing Yeshua.*
*The Tav, once shaped like a cross, was the final letter.*
*The last mark. The seal.* **YHWH was always Yeshua.**

The *dawn* is here.

# Table of Contents

Title Page……………………………………………i
Copyright……………………………………………ii
Dedication…………………………………………iii
Author's Note……………………………………..vii
Table of Contents………………………………….xi
Scripture Page…………………………………….xii
Prologue……………………………………………xv

**Part I – The Ache of Being Awake**
1. God, Why Do They Win?………………………1
2. I Can't Stop Asking, Even When I Know He Won't Stop It All………………………..5
3. The Suffering Seer………………………..11
4. The Hidden Ones…………………………..15
5. To Those Who Hear Differently………..19
6. I Know What I'd Do, And It Hurts…….23
7. When I Am Barely Breathing…………..29
8. The Ones Who Almost Gave Up………45
9. The Ache for the New Creation………..53
10. The Ache to Restore Eden……………...57
11. The Illusion of Protection………………61
12. What Will You Really Lose?………..…67

**Part II – Revelation in the Wilderness**

13. Why Is It Always Yeshua?...........................71
14. The Truth Beneath the gods...................77
15. Bring It All Because I Know Who Holds Me
...................................................................83
16. Set Me Ablaze.........................................89
17. The Altar of the Undivided...................93
18. The Ones Marked by Fire....................99
19. The Cry for the Sword........................103
20. The True Meaning of Dominion...........107

**Part III – The Light Before the Break**

21. The Empty Vessel...............................111
22. A Soul Blamed...................................117
23. Yirah..................................................119
24. Drawn Back to Propel Forward.............125
25. The Key to Happiness.........................129
26. I am Sahar: Dawn...............................133
27. To the One Who Stayed Until the End.....137
Epilogue: The Last Cry Before the Break.......141
Postlude: The Dawn. A Meditation..............147
Author's Final Note....................................151
Acknowledgments......................................153
About the Author......................................155
Connect with the Author..........................159
Final Scripture Seal...................................163
Notes.......................................................165

*I AM WHO I AM.*

—Exodus 3:14

*Before Abraham was,* **I AM.**

—John 8:58

*I am the **Aleph** and the **Tav**, says the YHWH, "*

*the One **who is**, and **who was**,*

*and **who is to come**,*

*the **Almighty**."*

—Revelation 1:8

# Prologue

You there—
yes, you with the ache that never quiets.

You who lie awake
long after the world has gone dim,
asking questions too heavy for your own chest
to carry.

You who've whispered into the ceiling,
*"God, why does it feel like You do not exist?"*

I know your silence.

I've sat in it too long to pretend it isn't real.
I've cried prayers that never got answers.
I've sat in the hollow space
between suffering and sovereignty
where logic fails
and only longing remains.

This book isn't for the ones
who've never doubted.
This isn't for the ones who live on stages

and quote clichés to silence real pain.

This is for the ones who almost gave up.
This is for the ones who screamed
and still weren't heard.
This is for the ones who feel too much
and ask too many questions.
This is for the ones who've seen
too much darkness
to believe in plastic light.

You are not weak for aching.
You are not foolish for questioning.
You are not alone for wondering
if you were left behind.

This world is cracked.
And sometimes, all you have is breath
and questions.
But even in that breath,
there is a Name.

Not a religion.
Not a system.
Not a Sunday routine.

But a Name older than time,

# Prologue

You there—
yes, you with the ache that never quiets.

You who lie awake
long after the world has gone dim,
asking questions too heavy for your own chest
to carry.

You who've whispered into the ceiling,
*"God, why does it feel like You do not exist?"*

I know your silence.

I've sat in it too long to pretend it isn't real.
I've cried prayers that never got answers.
I've sat in the hollow space
between suffering and sovereignty
where logic fails
and only longing remains.

This book isn't for the ones
who've never doubted.
This isn't for the ones who live on stages

and quote clichés to silence real pain.

This is for the ones who almost gave up.
This is for the ones who screamed
and still weren't heard.
This is for the ones who feel too much
and ask too many questions.
This is for the ones who've seen
too much darkness
to believe in plastic light.

You are not weak for aching.
You are not foolish for questioning.
You are not alone for wondering
if you were left behind.

This world is cracked.
And sometimes, all you have is breath
and questions.
But even in that breath,
there is a Name.

Not a religion.
Not a system.
Not a Sunday routine.

But a Name older than time,

more solid than death,
and so holy that even silence bows to it.

You may not know Him yet.
You may not even believe this Name matters.
But something in you is still reading,
still hungry,
still hoping that all of this
isn't for nothing.

That hope is not weakness.
It's a flicker.
And this book is a match.

So if you've ever wondered where He is,
if He sees you,
if He hears you,
if He could possibly be real in a world this cruel,

then walk with me.
You don't need to believe it all yet.
You just need to bring your ache.

I'll meet you there.

# Chapter 1: "God, Why Do They Win?"
*A Lament*

The ones who mock You,
laugh louder.
The ones who curse You,
seem to sleep better.
The ones who deny You,
are the ones You still let rise.

And here I am,
knees on the ground,
prayers in the dark,
tears in the pillow.

I tried to obey.
I tried to please You.
I tried to do what was right,
even when it broke me.

So why does it feel
like those who ignore You
get everything I've cried for?

Why do the arrogant prosper

while the faithful fall?

Why do I have to keep breathing
in the stench of this wicked world,
a world that delights in crushing the innocent
and elevating the cruel?

I hate it.
I hate every corner of it.

Why do You feel closer to the wicked
than to the weary who call Your Name?

I don't want vengeance.
I want understanding.

I'm not questioning Your holiness.
I'm questioning why holiness hurts this much.

If I'm Your child,
why do You feel like a stranger?

And if this is Your plan,
why does it feel like silence
dressed as sovereignty?

Please,

just tell me You see this.
Because I'm tired of feeling unseen
by the God I gave everything for.

Why do You make me feel
the pain of others so deeply,
but not let me do anything about it?

Why do You flood me with
fire in my bones
when I see the innocent crushed,
but then tell me to stay still?

Why give me eyes that see
the ones who pierce the young,
but not a sword to stop them?

Why must I be the vessel
for wounds I didn't cause?

Why do I weep for what they ignore?
Why do I carry agony I can't avenge?

If I could..
I would slash with justice,
I would roar with truth,
but You ask me only to pray.

You make me feel too much
to do so little.

And still, I obey.
But God,
it hurts to be this tender
in a world this cruel.

## Chapter 2: I Can't Stop Asking, Even When I Know He Won't Stop It All
*Why I Still Beg for the Innocent,
Even If It Hurts*

There are things I know in my mind:
truths I've learned through Scripture,
through experience,
through silence.

I know God doesn't always answer every
prayer
the way I want.
I know this world is fallen.
I know not every child is saved.
Not every animal escapes.
Not every horror is stopped.

But even knowing all that,
I still ask.

Every single time I witness pain,
especially in children or animals,
something in me rises
and refuses to look away.

It won't allow me to brush it off
as "Just part of the fallen world."
It just won't let me accept it.

Instead,
I fall into a kind of intercession
I never asked for:
a weeping,
aching,
full-body cry to YHWH
that may sound like desperation,
but is actually
love refusing to go numb.

I tell Him:

"Please stop it.
Please save them.
Please don't let that dog endure pain.
Don't let that baby suffer.
Don't let them be taken,
or slaughtered,
or forgotten.
Please. Stop it. End it."

I pray these things even when I know the
answer won't be yes.
Even when I know the suffering will continue,
and I'll still see it again tomorrow.
Even when it feels like God won't intervene
the way I'm begging Him to.

But I ask anyway.
And I can't stop.
I just… cannot.

I used to wonder if that made me broken.
Too sensitive.
Too emotional.
Or even unfaithful
for asking things I "should know better" about.

But the truth is this:
I was made this way on purpose.

I can't help that I carry the weight of suffering
in my chest.
I can't help that a video of a crying dog feels like
my own soul is being crushed.
I can't help that I avoid the endless stream
of media,
because the slightest sound of real pain

and suffering
makes my whole-body tremble.

But maybe that's not a curse.
Maybe it's the evidence
that YHWH still lives in me.

I carry the echo of Eden.

That's the only way I can explain it.
Something in me recognizes what the world
was supposed to be,
and what I yearn it to be,
before the blood,
before the screams,
before the fear.

And so when I see those things now,
I can't bear it.
Not because I'm too *soft*.
But because I'm not hardened
like the rest of the world.

That's a painful gift.
A heavy one.
But it's also set-apart.

So no,
I don't stop asking.

I still beg for the ones who can't speak.
For the animals trembling in cages.
For the children stolen and silenced.

Because even if the prayers aren't answered now,
they are not wasted.

They rise like incense.
They fill the bowls of Heaven.
They reach the heart of the YHWH
who was first pierced and wept, too.

And one day, when all is restored,
when the lion lies down with the lamb,
when the forest breathes again,
when the redeemed babies are safe forever,
and the redeemed dogs are no longer in pain,

I will know that I didn't stay silent.
I begged, even when it hurt.
And He will remember it,

for He is *El Roi*,
the One who sees the seen,
and the unseen,

          and *El Shaphat*,

            the One

        who renders justice

           righteously

         and eternally.

# Chapter 3: The Suffering Seer

I never asked to see this much.
I never asked to feel the grief that wasn't mine,
or carry sorrows that didn't belong to me.

But somehow, I do.

And I've come to understand
this is what it means to be a seer.
Not someone who tells the future.
But someone who feels the present
too deeply to ignore.

Someone who discerns the unseen pain
beneath the surface smiles.
Someone who cannot be numbed
even when it would be easier.

I've tried to run from it.
To shut it off.
To numb myself
like the rest of the world.

But He didn't let me.

Because He didn't design me
for numbness.

He designed me to feel,
so that others could begin to heal.

He gave me eyes to see through the veil:
not so I could boast in insight,
but so I could fall to my knees
for the things that others ignore.

It's not glamorous.
It's not easy.
It's not safe.

But it's set apart.
Because He is the One who sees all.
And if He lives in me,
then I will see what He sees
even when it breaks me.

The world might say I'm "too much."
Too intense.
Too sensitive.
Too aware.

But the Spirit whispers back:

"You were never too much for Me.
You were made to carry what others can't.
You were formed to feel what others won't.
Because someone needs to stand in the gap."

So I do.
And it hurts.
But I would rather hurt with Him,
than live numb without Him.

*The Tav, once shaped like a cross,*
*marked those who carried what others could not:*
*to see, to ache, to intercede.*
*It is the seal of the suffering ones*
*who walk with Him.*

14

## Chapter 4: The Hidden Ones

You may not have called yourself this way
before.
You may not have even known
there was a name for it.

But if you've ever felt too quiet to be noticed,
too intense to be accepted,
too different to fit the "mold" —
this might be for you.

Because there are more of us than you think.
And He has never overlooked us.

They don't talk about us.
We are the ones who don't show up in pulpits,
but we pray behind closed doors.

We are the ones who cry in silence,
but heaven hears our weeping.

We are the *quiet* ones:
the *misfits*,
the *outliers*,

the *strange* ones
who never quite belonged anywhere,
but still never stopped believing.

We walk through rooms unseen,
yet angels mark our every step.

We don't have microphones or stages,
but we carry messages in our bones.

We are the hidden ones.
And we were never meant to be center stage.

Because we are the ones who've been kept
for something set apart.

Something that can't be done in the spotlight.
Something that requires wilderness.
Something that only survives in secret places.

Like a seed buried deep
before it breaks open into life.

We're the ones who feel the Spirit move
before anyone else notices.
The ones who see shifts in the atmosphere
long before the world catches up.

Not because we're better.
But because we were broken early
and it made us sensitive enough to hear.

They say we're "too intense,"
"too sensitive,"
"too deep."
But that's exactly what makes us ready
and more self-aware,
and more aware of what's happening around us.

Ready for revival.
Ready for revelation.
Ready for the return of the King.

Because we've been refined by fire.
Stripped of applause.
Set apart—on purpose.

YHWH hides what He treasures.
He conceals what's not yet ready.
And He raises His hidden ones
in silence,
in sorrow,
in sacred training.

So if you feel unseen,
you might just be in hiding
because you're His.

And when the time comes,
you won't need to force a door open.
He will open it Himself.

Because the hidden ones
were never overlooked by Him.
Only preserved for His glory.

הוָה מָגִנֵּנוּ

**YHWH Maginnēnu**

YHWH our Shield,

the One who hides

and preserves His own.

# Chapter 5: To Those Who Hear Differently

This is for you:
the one who hears what others don't.

You notice when a smile
doesn't match their spirit.
You feel a shift in the room
before anyone speaks.
You cry when others stay numb.
You dream vividly,
and sometimes wake up knowing things
you can't explain.

You don't know how to say it
without sounding strange,
so you stay quiet.
You question yourself.
You doubt your discernment.
But deep down, you know.

You've always known.

You hear differently

because you were designed that way.
Not for confusion
but for calling.

The world calls it anxiety.
Overthinking.
Hyper-awareness.

But what if it's not a disorder—
what if it's a gift?

A gift that only functions
when it's surrendered to the One
who made you.

You were never meant to carry
this sensitivity alone.
You were never meant to bear the weight
of insight without guidance.

He didn't make you to suffer under this sight.
He made you to follow His voice with it.

You were made to tune into the frequency
of Heaven,
even if the world thinks you're just "too much."

You're not too much.
You're just not for this world's rhythm.
You were wired for a different sound.
A different cadence.
A different Kingdom.

And you're not crazy for hearing it.

So don't shut it down.
Don't numb it.
Don't let the world explain it away.

Bring it to the One who gave it to you.
Let Him train it.
Let Him lead it.
Let Him speak through it.

Because one day,
those who mocked your insight
will come to you for clarity.

And the voice you were once ashamed of
will be the very echo of the One
they didn't know they needed.

Because the voice was never yours alone.
It was always His.

יְהוָה רֹעִי

**YHWH Ro'i**

YHWH my Shepherd,

the One who trains my hearing

and leads me in His voice.

# Chapter 6: I Know What I'd Do, And It Hurts

Since I was young, I noticed I thought deeper
than those around me
While others talked about the surface,
I felt things more intensely.
I matured faster
in how I saw and understood the world.

Over time, I came to realize:
I wasn't just highly sensitive.
I was richly emotionally intelligent.
And beneath that, there was something deeper still.
A discernment that couldn't have come
from me alone.

Because every single day, I feel the weight of a
truth I can't escape:
I wouldn't just comfort the hurting,
I would rescue them.
I would end their pain.
I would pull the dogs from cages…
all of them.

I would tear down the systems that use forceps
to slaughter babies
and silence justice.
I would intervene
not just for one,
but for the multitudes.

If I had the resources, I wouldn't stop.
I would eradicate the "Dog Eating Festival"
permanently.
I would burn down every underground space
that hides a child for red rooms or the dark web.

I would be relentless.

But I don't.
I can't.
And that's the part no one really understands.

It's not just that I'm sensitive.
It's that I'm powerless
while still fully awake to the horror.

I don't want to just feel.
I want to act.

I don't want to only pray.

I want to intervene.

But right now?
I cry.
I beg.
I plead with God.

And I still watch the animals die.
I still see children suffer.
And I know, I help here and there,
with the little we have,
including prayers with tears

But when they're miles away,
when the need is vast and relentless,
I feel the ache of what I can't do
and the yearning to do so much more
than anyone would think.

That is what tortures me.
Because sometimes,
the pain of feeling is so intense that
I don't want to live anymore.

Does that make me weak?
Absolutely not.
It signifies a heart

that refuses to go numb,
that refuses to join the world's apathy,
to look away from suffering
like the evil ones do.

This ache is not a flaw.
It is a mark that YHWH's heart
is imbued in me,
and in others who ache just as fiercely.

So what's the point of all this feeling,
all this ache and pain?

What's the use of having this heart
if I can't use it to protect,
to rescue,
to change lives?

What's the use of being the person who would
give everything
if I have nothing to give?

It starts to feel like a kind of punishment.
A kind of cruel design
to see and feel so deeply,
but sit in silence,
unable to act.

And yes, I've asked God.
I've told Him:
"Why did You make me this way
if You weren't going to give me the means
to help?"

Because the pain of feeling
is too much when you're helpless.

And I'm not asking for comfort.
I'm not asking to 'feel better.'
I'm asking to do something,
to act,
to change,
to rescue.
And it hurts to know that I can't.

Not yet.

So yes.
I know what I'd do
if I had the resources,
the power,
the capacity
to turn every ache into action.

And that's why I cry the way I do.
That's why I avoid videos,
avoid scrolling,
avoid the things most people
ignore effortlessly.

Because I can't ignore them.
But I also can't fix them.

And that is where the pain lives:
In the chasm between my deep love
and my current limits.

יְהוָה צְבָאוֹת

**YHWH Tzeva'ot**

YHWH of Hosts,

the One who fights for the innocent

and leads His warriors

in His time.

## Chapter 7: When I Am Barely Breathing

Why must I be so broken
before I see You move?

Why must I lose my last breath
before I hear Yours draw near?

It feels sometimes
that only at the cliff edge of despair
does the wind shift.

Only when my heart falls silent in sorrow
do I hear the echo of Your footsteps.

I have begun to fear my own strength
for when I am strong,
I barely see You.

But when I am empty,
gasping,
and undone—
there, there You are.

Sometimes I wonder

if I must live forever on the edge
just to taste You.

But You are not only the God
who meets me in the pit.
You are the God who pulls me out of it.
When I was enslaved to the grind,
crying out to be freed from a place
that drained my soul,
You shattered the chains,
closed the doors,
and led me to the unknown.

And though it felt like loss to others,
it was Your merciful hand
rescuing me
from what I could not leave
on my own.

You are the God who breathes life in the heights.
You are the God of the valley,
and the mountaintop.
Because even in *Sheol*—
You are there.

Teach me to see Your hand

not only when I collapse,
but when I still have the strength
to reach for You.

Maybe one day
I'll be trusted with the means.
Maybe one day
I'll rescue the dogs,
the orcas,
the children.
Maybe one day I won't just pray —
I'll act.

But for now?

All I have is this ache.

This unbearable knowing.
This fire inside
would save the world,
if only it had hands strong enough,
or resources wide enough,
to do it.

And until then,
I just carry it.
Not because I want to…

but because I was made to.

Why is it that those who wounded me in youth,
and those who crushed me in later years,
still walk freely
while I carry the weight of every scar
they left behind?

Why has my life become a long road
of unanswered prayers,
a landscape where old hopes turn to ashes?

Why do I feel bound inside a story
I cannot rewrite?

I have stretched my hands toward better days,
but no doors open.
No winds shift.
No mercy falls.

Why must I stand year after year
in a wilderness that shows
no sign of ending?

Loneliness has carved itself into my bones,
a silence I know too well.
Sadness lingers at every doorway.

There are no close companions,
no voices steady enough to hold the weight
of unseen battles.

Why must the ones who broke me prosper,
while I bear the ruins alone?

I have cried for mercy.
I have pleaded for revival
even as dry bones gather dust
beneath my weary steps.

You breathed life once before
into graves,
into exiles,
into scattered ruins.

Why not here?
Why not now?

Why the silence?
Why the endless night?

I have pressed against the darkness.
I have begged for breath.

But still I remain
worn by deferred hopes,
aching in body,
aching in spirit.

Even my arms wear the heaviness
of unseen wars.

El Roi, who sees everything,
yet somehow
His forever eyes slip past me.

If all You allow are crumbs,
then I will gather them with open hands,
enough for me
and my children.  (Matthew 15:27-28)

It does not matter if I turn left or right,
the wilderness stays the same.

I don't know what else to do.

I keep trying.
I keep fighting.
I keep seeking You.

Even those near me

whisper and mock
after all my humbling,
the One still does not bow His chin
toward me.

I reach,
but the heavens remain unmoved.

I knock,
but the silence stays thick.

I wander forward with empty hands,
still hoping,
still breaking,
still waiting to be seen.

## When the Battle Never Ends
*(A Meditation on Living with Anxiety)*

There are wounds that don't bleed outside,
but they carve deep into your days.

Anxiety has lived with me for as long
like a shadow,
inseparable,

following me wherever I go.

It clings to me,
familiar,
yet unwanted,
casting its weight on every step.

Anxiety has shifted shapes over the years.
Some have lessened.
Others have grown stronger.

But the ache has always remained:
steady,
gnawing,
relentless.

The lingering trauma of how they treated me:
unspeakable nervousness and tension
clinging to me like a shadow,
arising from past wounds
and present unpredictability.

I am tired of carrying it.
Tired of walking with it.
Tired of waking up to a war
before I even open my eyes.
Tired of fighting battles

that never seem to end.

I hate it.
I want it gone.

Some days, it makes life feel pointless.
As if living under this weight
is just surviving,
not living at all

but just breathing…

## When Relief Betrays You
*(A Cry from the Deep)*

I just want it gone for good.
Can't You please just take it away?
Please. Please. Please.

When I thought I had finally found a
medication that felt like a heaven-sent answer,
then came the bloating,
the weight gain,
the sadness twisting tighter.

No matter what I ate,
or how little,
it left me bloated,
heavy,
and hollow inside.

It slowed my body so horribly
that it started slowing my heart, too.

Then came the next one.
Thought it was the one,
no bloating this time,
no dragging my heart down,
but it took my anxiety
and poured gasoline on it.

My heart raced
even in my sleep.

I couldn't win.
Whatever I tried,
nothing seemed to work.

I was so tired.
Tired of it all.

So I decided to quit.

I had to quit.
I had to find another way.

I'd lived my whole life without it—
so be it.

And hoping and begging
He would eliminate
every ounce if it from me.

I said: I'm done.
I'm just done with all this.

Maybe I'll just shelter myself,
stay safe where I can,
reduce my conflicts,
reduce my risks,
reduce my needs.
If that's even possible.

Maybe I'll just try.
Just try to live without it again.
Try to live inside the limits
I never asked for.

I don't know what else to do.
I'm tired of trying.

I'm tired of hoping.

I just want peace.
Real peace.
The kind that can't be taken away.

Is that too much to ask?


## When the Storm Pauses
*(A Cry for Quiet)*

As much as it aches me to release these words,
as much as I long to set this sorrow down,
I can't help but worry:

will I be putting You in a bad light?
Will my honesty…
give the mockers
another reason to jeer?

But You remind me
the right path is the narrow one.
And the narrow path
is the hardest road to walk on.

So if my way has been filled with sorrow,
if my steps have been bloodstained and lonely,
then perhaps
it is only confirmation
that I am still on the road
that leads home.

Still, even knowing that,
I can't deny it:
I ache for a break.
A breath.
A softening.

I long for the moment
when chaos finally quiets,
when thunder fades
into a low hush,
exhausted hush,
when the roaring waves pull back into the sea,
leaving only soft whispers
of water on the shore.

I long for the moment
when the fierce, unseen winds—
those that pierce through every defense—
finally surrender.
Not in defeat,

but in a tender dance,
rising softly into the sky
like a farewell.

I am not asking for a life without storms.
I am asking for the eye,
the center of the storm,
even if only for a moment
where I can lift my face without flinching,
where the battle pauses
just long enough
for me to breathe again.

## Whispering Toward Home
*(The Final Longing)*

Home.
That word echoes in me like a prayer.

Not the house I live in.
Not even the earth I walk across daily.
But the real Home.

The place beyond this body,
beyond this anguish,
beyond the battles that never seem to end.

Home.
Where sorrow finally loses its voice.
Where fear becomes a ghost of a forgotten story.
Where weariness is swallowed in eternal light.

I wish.
I pray,
that Home is closer than we think.

Closer than the miles.
Closer than the endless nights make it seem.
Closer even than my next breath.

Sometimes I wonder,
what if it's just around the bend?
What if Home is not distant,
but already approaching,
already coming nearer,
already brushing the edges of my brokenness?

I ache for that nearness.
I ache for the end of wandering.
I ache for the fierce winds to still,
and for the gates, gleaming like pearl,
to open wide
and call my name

finally, finally.

Until then,
I keep walking.
Still aching.
Still reaching.
Still believing
even in the dark
that Home is nearer than it feels.

יהוה נִסִּי

**YHWH Nissi**

YHWH my Banner,

the One under whose covering

I keep walking until the battle end.

# Chapter 8: The Ones Who Almost Gave Up

They look like everyone else
but inside, they're already gone.

They go through the motions.
They show up.
They smile.
They nod when someone says, "God is good."
But inside? They're emptied.

They are the ones who almost gave up.
And maybe… they still might.

Not because they don't love God,
but because the pain He let them carry
has worn their love thin.

Not because they stopped believing,
but because belief hasn't stopped the ache.

These are the ones who prayed the hardest
and still watched the worst happen.

The ones who gave everything
and still lost what they begged Him to save.

The ones who fasted,
cried,
obeyed,
but heard only silence in return.

These are the ones who whisper in the dark,
"If You don't come through soon…
I don't know how much more I can hold."

I know them.
Because I am them.

I've stood on the edge of quitting
not just life,
but hope.

I've stared at the ceiling and said,
"Why did You keep me breathing
if You won't show me why I'm still here?"

But somehow,
every time I near the edge,
something deeper rises.

Not strength.
Not optimism.
Not a fake kind of faith

Not a forced smile.
But a flicker.

A flicker of a God who sees.
A God who remembers.
A God who lets me feel the end
just so He can show me
it's not over.

And that flicker
is what keeps me breathing.

To the ones who almost gave up:
I see you.
But more importantly,
He sees you.

He didn't stop the pain, I know.
But He also didn't walk away.

He's still here.
Still listening.
Still waiting for the moment you'll say,

"I'm not giving up
even if I don't understand."

Because that's when the flicker becomes flame.
The flame becomes fire.
And the fire becomes purpose.

Stay.

Even if it feels like you're standing in ashes.
Even if your hands are empty.
Even if your heart is shattered.

Stay.

Because He's not done yet.
Not with you.
Not with this story.

You are the ones who almost gave up
but didn't.
Not just once,
but many times.

Not in a dramatic way.
Not with announcements or noise.
But in quiet ways:

the kind of almost-giving-up that creeps in
when you're alone in the shower,
or staring at the ceiling at 3 a.m.,
whispering, "What's the point?"
And the silence answers back, nothing.

Stay.

You've smiled through breakdowns.
You've served while feeling empty.
You've kept showing up
even when you didn't know why.

You didn't lose faith.
But you lost the will to keep hoping.

And yet…
somehow you stayed.

Somehow you didn't disappear.
Somehow your feet kept walking,
even when your heart was limping.

Stay.

You never got applause for it.
No one clapped for the moment

you chose not to quit.
No one saw the days you didn't want to live,
but still lived anyway.

You're the ones who will shine brightest
when the veil is lifted.

Because the ones who almost gave up
didn't carry a glory
this world can't recognize.

The ones who stayed
even when staying felt like dying
will be the first to see the King's face
when He returns.

And He remembers that.
Not with pity
but with purpose.

Because your story isn't something to hide.
It's a weapon forged in silence.

And soon,
what once made you ache
will become the fire that wakes others up.

You weren't overlooked.
You were being prepared.
For such a time as this.

Now rise.

Because someone's breakthrough depends
on your survival.

Because when you broke,
you didn't let go of Him.

And now,
He will never let go of you.

יְהוָה שָׁמָּה,

For He is

**YHWH Shammah,**

the One

who is always there.

# Chapter 9: The Ache for the New Creation
*A Cry for the End of Suffering
and Creation's Redemption*

I'm tired of hearing the cries of animals,
harmed, abused, slaughtered.
Tired of the wails of innocence shattered,
of children whose delicate bodies,
delicate minds,
delicate souls,
are crushed by a world without mercy.

I cannot wait any longer.
I am straining for the surface
like a soul trapped deep in the dark ocean,
swimming upward as fast as I can,
holding my breath,
desperate to break through
and finally gasp for air.

But deep inside, I fear
the road is still long.
The surface is still far away.

And all I can do is look away,
refuse to stare too long into the brokenness,
protect what little strength remains.
Because I cannot bear it.

I want to smite the destroyers.
I want to shield the innocent.
I want to tear apart the hands that harm.
But You have not given me that sword.

You have only given me tears.
You have only given me prayers.
You have only asked me to endure.

And I am tired.
So, so tired.

I ache for the new world You promised.
I ache for cruelty's roar to finally fall silent.
I ache for the lion to lie with the lamb,
for the cries of the broken to cease,
for the waters of suffering to part forever.

I ache for the dawn that never ends.

And until then,
I carry this unbearable longing

because You have made me feel it,
because You have made me see it—
the world that is not yet healed.

And still I wait.
Still I swim upward.
Still I pray for the day
when breath will no longer be a battle,
but a gift—fully given at last.

You said that we would live to see it:
the lion lying with the lamb,
the sun and moon no longer needed,
because Your glory would be the only light.
The only lamp.

And I said,
all creation, not just mankind.

All of it healed.
All of it whole.
All of it at peace again.

I long for it.
How I ache for it
How I strain for it.

*For the eager longing of the creation waits*

*for the revealing of the sons of Elohim.*

*For the creation was subjected to futility,*

*not willingly,*

*but because of Him who subjected it,*

*in hope that the creation itself*

*also shall be delivered from the bondage*

*to corruption into the esteemed freedom*

*of the children of Elohim.*

*For we know that all the creation*

*groans together, and suffers*

*the pains of childbirth together until now.*

—Romans 8:19-22

Greek: στενάζει, *(stenazei)*
to groan, sigh deeply,
express grief
or longing from within

# Chapter 10: The Ache to Restore Eden
*A Cry for What Was Lost*

I don't want power.
I want restoration.

I don't want to rule.
I want to rebuild.

The ache in me isn't for dominance.
It's for the return of what was lost:
The garden.
The stillness.
The intimacy with God
without veil,
without shame.

I wasn't made for this broken world.
None of us were.

And maybe that's why it hurts so much
to live in it,
because somewhere in our spirits,
we still ache for the Eden we've never known,

Not in detail,
but in essence
in the way our spirits groan with creation,
longing for what YHWH once called
"very good."

In the way our hearts recoil at cruelty.
In the way we grieve
without knowing the reason.
In the way our souls cry out,
*"This is not how it was meant to be."*

I feel it in my bones,
the ache to restore the innocence,
the hunger for harmony,
the desperate longing
for the curse to break.

I wasn't called to dominate.
I was called to liberate what I can
through tears,
through tenderness,
through being the opposite
of what corrupted Eden in the first place.

I don't want to win.
I want to heal.

I want to walk with Him
in the cool of the day.
I want to see the lion rest beside the lamb.
I want to dwell in the place
where no tear ever falls.

I can't do that yet.
But He can.

And so, I align with Him.
I follow the One
who is the Author of Eden,
the Tree of Life,
the Restorer of all things.

The ache in me isn't just pain.
It's prophecy.

A longing that will one day be fulfilled.
Because He said
He would make
*all things new.*

*And Elohim shall wipe away every tear*
*from their eyes,*
*and there shall be no more death,*
*nor mourning,*
*nor crying,*
*and there shall be no more pain,*
*for the former things have passed away.*

—Revelation 21:4

# Chapter 11: The Illusion of Protection
*The Only True Protection*

We say we want to protect our loved ones.

We build fences,
set rules,
install cameras,
lock doors,
track locations.

We do everything we can to shield them
because love feels like protection.

And sometimes, it works.
Until it doesn't.

Because one day,
something slips past our fences.
Something crawls through the cracks.

And the truth stares us in the face:

We were never in control.

And that is the most terrifying
and freeing
revelation of all.

Because if I can't fully protect the ones I love,
if my hands aren't big enough,
strong enough,
fast enough,

then maybe they were never meant
to rest in my hands at all.

Maybe the ache for protection is sacred.

Maybe it was meant
to lead me to the only One who truly can.

I used to think being a good mother meant
guarding every outcome.
I thought it meant being everywhere,
knowing everything,
planning for every threat.

But I've learned something deeper.

There was a night
I don't remember the time,

but I can never forget the moment.

I was asleep beside my infant,
arms wrapped around her small body,
holding her close.

And then
something woke me.

Not a sound.
Not a cry.
But a sudden, urgent knowing.

My whole body jolted awake,
spirit and flesh,
eyes wide open.

And in that split second,
I saw her,
my baby at the edge of the bed,
just about to fall.

Another heartbeat,
another second,
and she would have hit the floor.

But that waking,

that silent alarm,
that unspoken shout
from somewhere beyond me,
it saved her.

It wasn't a noise.
It wasn't my own intuition.
It was a Presence,
Merciful and near,
Who saw what I couldn't.

*YHWH Shammah,*
the One who is there.
*El Roi,*
the One who sees.

And I wept,
not only because she was safe,
but because He was that near,
nearer than my human wisdom
could ever fathom.

The One whose flame that never flickers.
The Shield that never shatters.
The Presence that sees before danger rises
and stands where no human can.

It's not my strength that keeps my children safe.
It's my surrender.

Surrender to the One
who formed them
in the womb.
Surrender to the One
who wrote their days
before I even held them.
Surrender to the One
who loves them
more than I ever could.

This is the only true protection:
Not control.
Not paranoia.
Not power.

But proximity
to the One who holds eternity.

The I AM is the protection
we were always searching for.

And when we entrust our lives,
our families into His hands,
we do not lose control.

We gain peace
that the world cannot give,
and faith
that the world cannot describe
in human language.

*He who dwells in the secret place of Elyon*

*will abide under the shadow of Shaddai.*

*I will say of YHWH,*

*"My refuge and my fortress,*

*My Elohim, in whom I trust."*

—Psalm 91:1-2

## Chapter 12: What Will You Really Lose?
*A Wake-Up Cry*

People ask why pain exists.
Why heartbreak shows up in the innocent.
Why betrayal comes to the loyal.
Why chaos finds the quiet.

Why do the ones who try to live rightly
still get crushed?
Why does the ache come
even when we're not looking for it?

But maybe that's not the right question.

Maybe the real question is:
what is the pain trying to reveal?

Could it be that you were never meant
to live without Him?
Could it be that your soul is screaming
for something this world cannot offer?

We try to make sense of a world unraveling
by clinging tighter to it.

We hold onto false peace.
False control.
False security.
False purpose.

But what if the loss is really
the beginning of light?
What if your suffering isn't proof
that God has left
but proof that He's trying to break through?

You weren't meant to carry this alone.
You weren't designed to be your own savior.
You were not built to protect yourself,
rescue yourself,
or even heal yourself.

You were made to know the Uncreated One:
The One who is YHWH in full.
The I AM in flesh.
The Consuming Fire,
the indestructible Fortress,
the First and the Last.

He is not a religion.
He is not a story.
He is the Truth that cannot be split.

The Way that cannot be replaced.
The Life that cannot be stolen.

So what is it that you are too afraid to lose?

Your money?
Your image?
Your applause?
Your place in a broken world?
Your version of control?

You cannot lose what was never meant to last.

But you can gain what will never die.
Peace that is not circumstantial.
Love that does not betray.
Protection that does not weaken.
Truth that does not shift.

And life,
true Life
that does not end
when your body does.

You say you want answers.
But are you willing to receive the Answer
who doesn't fit in your box?

You say you want peace.
But are you ready to lay down the pieces
that don't belong in your temporary hands?

You say you want protection.
But have you met the One
who holds the countless stars in His breath
and still cares about your tears?

The Uncreated One is not one of many.
He is the **Only.**

The Only Truth.
The Only Door.
The Only Name that saves.
The Only Love that will not fail.

So again, I ask you:
what will you really lose?

Because all I see
is proof
that you were created
to receive Everything.

# Chapter 13: Why Is It Always Yeshua?
*The Authority That Cannot Be Imitated*

Have you ever noticed
in every case of demonic possession,
in the most terrifying moments of darkness
when evil fully reveal itself,
when the darkness is no longer hidden,

when possession or torment becomes
undeniable
no other name holds the same weight.

People call on many names.
Buddha, Muhammad, crystals, energy, light,
even the created universe,
but the darkness does not tremble.

Only one Name makes demons flee.
Only one Name exposes evil for what it is.
Only one Name forces the unseen to bow.

Even those who don't believe,
even the ones who mock Him
when the darkness becomes too real,
when the evil is no longer abstract,

they scream for the one they hope
is real enough to save them.

There is a Name that cannot be ignored.

But Only One has the authority.
Only One is not created.
Because **He alone is the Creator.**

Demons don't tremble at any other name.
They don't beg to be left alone
by "energy" or "light."

They tremble at Him.
They scream in agony when He is near.
Because they know.

They know His Name
is above every name.

They know He is not just a prophet,
not just a teacher.

They know He is not one
among many.

They know **He is YHWH.**

The **Ancient of Days.**
The **First** and the **Last.**
The **I AM.**

He is the Living God.
He is the Consuming Fire
that no evil can endure.

He is the Word
that existed before all things.
He is the One who walked among us
not as a messenger,
but as the Message itself.

So why is it always Y…..?

Because every knee will bow.
Whether by love or by fear,
whether in life or in death,
whether in belief or in resistance,

every knee will bow
and every tongue will confess
that **Y….. is YHWH.**

Not just over humanity
but over all things seen and unseen.
Over every demon,
every watcher,
every spirit of darkness.

Even hell knows His voice.
Even the pit recognizes His footsteps.

There is only one Name
that makes the unseen tremble.
There is only one Truth
that cannot be copied.
There is only one Authority
that does not negotiate.

Because **He was never created.**
**He created all.**

He is the Judge.
He is the Lion and the Lamb.
He is both Righteous Wrath and Divine Mercy.
He is both the Taker and the Giver of Life.
The Judge and the Redeemer.

He is the Only One powerful enough
to quench all spirits

those from any level of heaven,
from the earth,
from the abyss,
and from under the earth.

And no spiritual power, prince, or authority
can escape His lightning sword.

He is…

# Yeshua

## *Melech haOlam*

## Ruler of the Universe

*So that at the name of Yeshua*

*every knee should bow,*

*in heaven and on earth and under the earth,*

*and every tongue confess that*

*Yeshua the Messiah is YHWH,*

*To the glory of Elohim the Father.*

—Philippians 2:10-11

## Chapter 14: The Truth Beneath the gods

Have you ever wondered?

Why every civilization across the earth
no matter how far apart
has always believed in gods?

Why every culture,
every era,
every ancient kingdom
carved stories into stone,
offered sacrifices,
bowed in temples,
lifted their eyes to something higher?

It's not coincidence.
It's not collective delusion.

It's a memory,
an echo,
etched into the human soul.
(Ecclesiastes 3:11)

Yes, there are gods.

But only One is God.
And deep inside,
every soul knows it.

You were never created
to kneel to shadows,
to replicas or counterfeit,
to limited created beings.
You were reverently made
to walk with Him.

He is Elohim.
He is YHWH.
He is Yeshua—
*Ehyeh Asher Ehyeh.*

**The I AM that I AM.**

Even the fallen ones:
those beings once created
to serve the Most High
tremble at His Name.

They were not always wicked.
They were not always deceivers.

They were forged for glory

until pride swallowed their purpose whole.

And in their fall,
they dragged humanity
into the fog of confusion.

But no matter how many false gods rose,
No matter how many myths were born,
No matter how many temples were built
in their names,
there has always been
only One Creator.

You can't counterfeit what is already Eternal.

And that's why false gods exist
because they are distortions of a truth
mankind can't erase.

There is only one
who speaks creation into being.
Only one
who holds time and space in His hands.

Only one
who formed you in the secret place
and breathed eternity into your lungs.

There is no other name.

Not Buddha.
Not Krishna.
Not Horus.
Not Aliens.
Not the stars,
nor the moon,
nor the crystals buried in the dirt.

All of it—*created*.

But YHWH?
*Uncreated.*
Unmoved.
Unchanging.
Untouchable.

And Yeshua?
He is the image of the invisible God.
The Word made flesh.
The fullness of the I AM
dwelling among us.

So you must ask yourself:
Why are you afraid to face this?

Why cling to names
that never bled for you?

Why are you bowing to creation
when the Creator knew you
before you were even formed?
(Jeremiah 1:5)

It's not about religion.
It's not about tradition.

It's about Truth.

And truth has a Name.

You can reject Him.
You can resist Him.

But you can't replace Him.

Because Yeshua isn't one god among many.
He is the beginning and the end.
The first breath and the final word.

The flame that never goes out.

So look again.

Look past the idols.
Look past the confusion.
Look into the mirror of your own spirit and ask:

Who made me?
Who sustains me?

Who has the authority
to call me by name?

And when the answer echoes
through the depths of your soul,

don't look away.
Don't blink.

Don't run back to the comfort of confusion.

Because once you know the Truth,
you'll never be content with anything less.

You were never meant to kneel
to shadows.
You were made to walk
in the **Light.**

## Chapter 15: Bring It All Because I Know Who Holds Me
*For the One Who's Tired of Worrying*

You worry about judgment.
You worry about war.
You worry about pandemics.
You worry about your future.

You worry about your bank account.
You worry what people think.
You worry about being acknowledged, validated, seen.

You worry if you're successful enough.
If you're beautiful enough.
If you're good enough.
If you're enough—period.

You worry about calamity.
You worry about suffering.
You worry about the chaos coming,
the chaos already here.

You worry about the noise inside

and the world raging outside your door.

You worry and worry and worry.

But don't you know?

I tell you this.
Bring the war.
Bring the chaos.
Bring the empty bank account.
Bring the silence.
Bring the betrayal.
Bring the fear.
Bring the shattered dreams.
Bring the death of what life could have been.
Bring the night.
Bring the storm.

Because I serve the One who is unshakeable.
Indivisible.
Immovable.
Indestructible.
Inimitable.
Eternal.
Absolute.

I stand under the wings of the Most High,

*El Elyon, Elohim,*
and in His shadow,
there is no fear.

Let the world fall apart.
Let the safety be stripped.
Let the applause die down.
Let the labels fall off.
Let the comforts burn.

Because I am His.

And nothing can snatch me out of His hand.
(John 10:28)

Not death.
Not famine.
Not war.
Not betrayal.
Not shame.
Not failure.
Not even my past.

I am covered by Yeshua.
(Psalm 91:4, Matthew 23:37)
Not as a phrase
but as a promise fulfilled.

He is El Gibbor—Mighty God.
He is El Shaddai—All-Sufficient.
He is El Roi—All-Seeing God.
He is El Tzeva'ot—Commander of All Hosts.

He is Ehyeh Asher Ehyeh,
The I AM that I AM.

Not bound by time,
not shaken by man,
and not mocked by any living breath.
(Galatians 6:7)

So bring it all.
Bring the worst.
Bring the unraveling.

Because I will not stand in my strength.
I will stand in His.
And His alone.

And if you knew Him,
if you truly knew Him,
you would not fear what is to come.

Because once you are His, (Ephesians 1:13)

you are eternally sealed. (John 10:28-29)
You are eternally held.
You are eternally loved.

And nothing,
not the darkness, (Romans 8:38-39)
not the government,
not the devil himself
can change that.

So bring it all.

Because I am not afraid.
I only fear the One
who holds eternity in His hands,
who can destroy both the soul
and the body.
(Matthew 10:28)

# Chapter 16: Set Me Ablaze

*For Those Who Are Done Playing Lukewarm*

I'm not here to be balanced.
I'm not here to be moderate.
I'm not here to be liked.

I was not born for the middle ground.

I was born to burn.

Not with anger.
Not with chaos.
But with holy fire.

The kind that refuses to bow to culture.
The kind that silences lies with truth.
The kind that doesn't need applause
because it already hears
the voice of the I AM saying,
"Well done."

I wasn't made for lukewarm.
And neither were you.

Because you feel it too,
don't you?

That fire in your bones when injustice prevails.
That ache in your chest when truth is mocked.
That cry in your spirit that says,
"There has to be more than this shallow,
plastic version of 'faith'."

That's the fire.

That's the Spirit of the Living God
refusing to be silenced in you.

Don't quench it.
Don't tame it.
Don't apologize for it.

Let it roar.

Let it break the silence.
Let it rise in your prayers.
Let it pour from your pen.
Let it tremble the darkness
in every room you walk into.

You were not made to blend in.

You were not made to water Him down.

You were made to declare:
Yeshua is YHWH.

Not a prophet.
Not a moral teacher.
Not a second-hand reflection.

He is the I AM.

The One who appeared in the bush of fire.
The One who walked with the fourth man
in the furnace.
The One whose eyes are flames
and whose return will split the skies
like thunder.

This is not religion.
This is fire.
And if you don't feel it,
ask for it.
Cry out for it.

Let Him strike your heart like flint
until it sets the world ablaze.

Because the world doesn't need
another nice Christian.

It needs a burning one.
A true follower of Yeshua.

So let them say you're too intense.
Let them say you've changed.
Let them call it too much.

Because those that wait upon YHWH
will renew their strength.
They shall mount up with wings like eagles.
They shall run and not be weary.
They shall walk and not faint.
(Isaiah 40:31)

You're exactly where you're meant to be.
Set apart.
Set ablaze.
Ready to be consumed
with His purpose
and holy fire.

# Chapter 17: The Altar of the Undivided

There comes a moment when you realize
you don't just need a breakthrough.
You need a burning.

A place where everything false is consumed.
Where everything divided in you is laid bare.
Where every idol pretending to comfort you
is shattered under the weight of His name.

We've tried it all, haven't we?

Therapy without truth.
Healing without holiness.
Peace without repentance.
Spirituality without the Spirit.
Power without surrender.

But nothing satisfies.

Nothing fills the aching core.
Nothing restores what broke inside.
Nothing saves except One.

Yeshua.

Not as theory.
Not as symbol.

But as the living,
breathing,
consuming I AM.

You don't need another affirmation.
You need an altar.

You don't need more followers.
You need fire.

You don't need another distraction.
You need deliverance.

And it starts here,
at the altar
of the Undivided.

The place where your double-mind is healed.
The place where your half-love is exposed.
The place where your "almost obedience"
dies in the light of His holiness.

He is not asking for perfection.
He is looking for your yes.

Not your perfect yes.
Just your surrendered one.

So lay it down.
Lay it all down.

Your pride.
Your image.
Your need to be right.
Your "spiritual" labels.
Your fear of looking foolish.

Lay it all down until all that's left is this:

I am Yours. Undivided
even in my failing.

Let Him burn away what can't stay.
Let Him cleanse what shame tried to bury.
Let Him roar over every voice that told you
you were too much,
too late,
too unqualified,
too sinful,

too broken.

Because you are none of those things.
Once you're His,
He makes the unqualified **qualified,**
(2 Corinthians 3:5)
the late **early,** (Matthew 20:16)
the too much, **enough,** (Psalm 139:14)
the sinful, **redeemed,** (Ephesians 1:7)
the broken, **complete.** (Colossians 2:10)

You are **chosen.** (1Peter 2:9)
You are **called.** (Romans 8:30)
You are **fire-marked.** (Jeremiah 20:9)

And from this altar,
you will not walk away the same.

You will rise. (Isaiah 60:1)

Not perfect.
But **purified.** (Malachi 3:3)

Not loud.
But **burning.** (Luke 24:32)

Not famous.

But **faithful**. (Matthew 25:23)

Because the altar of the Undivided
doesn't just burn what's false,
it brands you as His.

And your name will be etched
in the *Lamb's Book of Life*.
(Revelation 3:5)

## Chapter 18: The Ones Marked by Fire

You who are reading this,
you are not here by accident.

You've walked through fire not just to survive,
but to be marked by it.

Not the world's fire.
But His.

Holy fire.
Refining fire.
The fire that does not destroy,
but defines.

You've wept in secret.
You've prayed in groans.
You've fought with no one cheering.

But He watched.

And now you stand,
not without scars
but with seal.

A seal that says:

*This one is Mine.*

You didn't chase applause.
You didn't crave titles.
You didn't build a brand.
You built an altar.

And the fire answered.

You're not like the others.
You were set apart long before you knew what that meant.

And now the time has come.

The wilderness shaped your voice.
The silence trained your ears.
The fire refined your hands.

So when the trumpet sounds,
you won't shrink back.
You'll rise.

Not to be seen.

But to speak.

Not to rule.
But to reveal.

Not to shine for yourself.
But to carry the Glory of the One
who dwells in unapproachable light.

And so, you who were once hidden,
arise!

Not loud.
But luminous.

Not perfect.
But pure.

Not many.
But mighty.

For this is the hour of the fire-bearers.
The seers.
The prophets.
The remnant.

The ones who do not flinch.

The ones who do not sell out.
The ones who burn with a love
that cannot be quenched.

You are not small.
You are not forgotten.
You are not disqualified.

You are marked.

And the world will not understand.
But Heaven already rejoices.

Go now:
carry the fire!

Let the altar burn in your bones
and the Spirit thunder from your mouth.
Let the world see
not your glory
but His,
through you.

For the time is short.
And the fire is rising.

## Chapter 19: The Cry for the Sword
*A Prayer of Fierce Longing*

Can't You?
Can't You please just allow me to have a sword?

And I don't mean a sword of words,
or patience,
or mercy.

I mean the sword:
the sword that strikes,
the sword that cuts down the cruel,
the sword that answers the cries of the broken
with swift justice.

You are the Sword.
You are the Flame.
But I long to hold it in my own hands
to wield it against those who destroy
without remorse.

I am not merciful like You.
And yet I understand You.

I understand why You destroy
what must be destroyed.
I understand why You allow pain
to come to those
who have inflicted pain on others.
I understand why You allow death
to reach those who snuffed out
the very breath You once gave.

I do not question You.
I see it.
I see You.

**El Gibbor**, Mighty God.
**El Roi**, the God who sees.

You are never mocked.
You are never fooled.
You do not forget the blood
spilled in secret.
You do not overlook the cries
that rise from hidden places.

You see the darkest corners.
You hear the muffled screams.
You measure the weight of every
unspoken sorrow.

And You are sharpening Your lightning sword,
honing it,
tempering it,
preparing it for the day of judgment.

The day when the hidden will be exposed.
The day when the arrogant will fall.
The day when every cruelty will be answered
by fire.

I understand.
I understand it all.

And still I ache to hold the sword now.
To be Your hand of justice now.
But I am not permitted yet.

So I stand
trembling,
burning,
waiting

for the day You rise,
for the day You unsheathe Your glory,
for the day You roar,
and the earth trembles in answer.

*Behold, He is coming with the clouds,*

*and every eye will see Him,*

*even those who pierced Him,*

*and all tribes of the earth will wail*

*on account of Him.*

*Yes. Amen.*

—Revelation 1:7

# Chapter 20: The True Meaning of Dominion
*A Cry to Rule with Mercy*

We were meant to rule them.

You created us to govern
the creatures of the earth,
but not as dictators,
not as abusers,
not as cruel masters.

You meant something far more beautiful.

In Hebrew, the word is רָדָה (radah[1]).
It does not mean domination.

It means rulership like a shepherd-king:
to guide,
to protect,
to tend,

---

[1] Radah (רָדָה): Hebrew for "to rule." It means to govern with care, protection, and responsibility, the way a shepherd lovingly guides his flock. It is rulership that mirrors the heart of the Creator, not domination.

to defend,
to love.

You entrusted creation to us,
not to exploit,
but to shelter.
Not to destroy,
but to nurture.

For You loved them first.

You breathed life into them.
You called them good.
You wove them into the tapestry of Eden.

You did not make us rulers to exploit
but to love, protect, and carry as sacred trust.

Even when Jonah tried to turn his back,
even when he fled from your mercy,
You spoke of Your compassion
not only for the people of Nineveh,
but for the animals too.

*"And should I not have concern*
*for the great city of Nineveh,*
*in which there are more than a hundred*
*and twenty thousand people*
*who cannot tell their right hand from their left,*
*and also many animals?"*
(Jonah 4:11)

You, my Elohim,
the Merciful One,
the Loving One,
the One who sees.

I see Your heart in this.
I understand what You meant from the beginning.

Oh, how I wish they could see You too:
to know Your heart,
to feel Your tenderness,
to understand Your justice,
to be undone by Your unshakeable love
for even the smallest of Your creations.

How I ache for the day when Your design will be restored.
When we will rule not with fists

but with hands that heal,
hands that build,
hands that bless.

When the world will finally understand what it
means to be made in Your image,
not to destroy,
but to protect.

Until that day,
I carry the ache
for Your heart to be known
in all the earth,
and among all the creatures
under heaven.

# Chapter 21: The Empty Vessel
*A Lament in the Waiting*

All my life,
all I do is fight,
fight,
fight.

It feels as if I am being dared
to spend every ounce of hope left in me,
to empty every drop of strength I have.

It feels as if heaven is waiting
for me to surrender,
to accept defeat.

But I am not that strong.
I am tired.
So tired.

Why must I keep fighting?
For what?

It all feels meaningless now.

I would rather sleep,
fall into a deep, deep sleep
where the ache of trying
can finally go silent.

Everything has lost its colour.
Everything has lost its meaning.

And even though You see this ache,
even though You hear this lament,
it is still not loud enough
to pierce You to move.

It seems my cries are nothing but noise.
A sound too small
to stir You.

And it doesn't matter what I do.
Whatever I try
to please You,
to reach You,
to move You,
it all ends the same.

Silence.
And more suffering.

I try to put a smile on Your face,
even though I do not know
if You ever smile back at me
for the things I tried to do
for *the least of these.*


## An Empty Vessel.

I was right about what I have felt all along:
I am an empty vessel.

An empty vessel,
awaiting its purpose,
not knowing its reason for existing,
sometimes feeling pointless
for even being here.

An empty vessel,
waiting to be filled by the Potter's hands.

I have pondered,
and though I could be wrong
that maybe once I was made beautiful,
crafted for a purpose.

But sin, dishonourable acts

broke me,
pushed me further away
from the Hands that formed me.

A broken vessel,
blocked from what was waiting,
clouded the path to its calling,
wandering aimlessly.

I, the vessel, was shattered into pieces.
Yet by the grace of the Potter,
this vessel, once broken,
was mended again.

I am whole,
but covered in scars.
I am standing,
but still empty.

And the question remains:

Will this mended vessel ever be beautiful again,
even with the scars?
Will this empty frame be filled to the brim,
and finally find its reason for being?
Will this vessel,
waiting and unseen,

one day be poured out
for *His glory*?

How long must I wait?
How long must the once-dishonourable vessel
stay empty,
longing to be used for honourable purposes?

I am still an empty vessel,
hoping,
waiting,
longing
to shine like the rest of the vessels
that seem full,
purpose-filled,
beautiful.

I am like a vessel:
a broken vase pieced back together,
standing in the midst of all the other beautiful
and distinct vases
in this great pottery room.

I alone stand out
not because I am the most beautiful,
but because I am the only one
who was shattered,

and then mended.

But for what?

All the others are distant from me.
They shine in their places,
sure of their meaning,
awaiting purposes that seem obvious
and certain.

But I?

I stand alone in the center of the room
wondering why I am still here at all.

Not awaiting,
not expecting,
just wondering.

Why am I still here,
when it might have been simpler for me
to disappear?

## Chapter 22: A Soul Blamed

I spoke my pain aloud,
but they heard only accusations against me.

"You are the trigger," they said.
"You are the cause of your own breaking."

As if my suffering was deserved.
As if the bruises in my spirit
were my fault alone.

They said there would be no happiness
for someone like me.

No one who would stay.
No one who would understand.

And if that is true,
then what is the point of carrying this heart
at all?

I have tried to shape myself
into something acceptable,
something understandable,

something lovable.

But I was not made to erase my soul.

And if the world demands it,
then perhaps I was never meant to belong here.

I am tired of trying to fit into places
that were never made to hold me.

Tired of breathing in a world
that never made room for souls like mine.

But the ache I carry
was never for them to understand
but was only to be known by You.

# Chapter 23: Yirah
*When Awe Becomes the Answer*

For a long time,
I lived beneath heavy skies.

I knew sadness intimately.
I knew silence.

I knew what it was to pray
without hearing anything back
to ache without any visible answer.

I cried out.
I fought.
I kept moving forward
through a wilderness that felt endless.

But then, something happened.
Something that changed everything.
Not by removing the suffering,
but by revealing something greater inside of it.

It didn't come with flashing signs.
It didn't come through a sudden miracle.

It came quietly
like a still, sharp fire in my chest.

A knowing.
An awe I had never truly touched before.

For the first time in my life,
I began to experience what Scripture calls
*yirah*[2] —
the fear of the Lord.
But not fear as terror.

*Yirah*, true, holy awe.
Trembling reverence.
A burning amazement too deep for words.

In those days,
something inside me was bursting open.
I became overwhelmed with who God really is,

---

[2] Yirah (יִרְאָה) is the Hebrew word often translated as "fear," but it means far more than terror. It speaks of holy awe, an overwhelming reverence, trembling wonder, and deep recognition of God's majesty. It is the soul's response when it truly beholds the glory of the I AM.

not who I had been taught,
not the distant idea,
but the Living Yahweh.

I began to realize that Yeshua is not just a messenger.
Not just a representation.
He is YHWH Himself.

The "888,"
the meaning of His Name,
the signs,
the patterns,
the affirmations,
they flooded my spirit,
confirming what my soul had already started to whisper:

Yeshua is the visible Image of the Invisible God.
The **I AM in flesh.**
The fullness unveiled.

I had lived for so long thinking I knew Him.
But I had only glimpsed a fraction.

Now, awe began to undo me.

I felt as though I might explode under the
weight of it.
The glory was too real,
too heavy to contain.

This wasn't imagination.
This wasn't emotionalism.

It was encounter.
A living experience of the One who has no rival,
no equal,
no shadow.

I had found the Treasure.
Or rather—
the Treasure had found me.

I had cried out for answers.
I had begged for healing.
I had asked for explanations.

What I received instead
was a revelation.

Not of why everything hurt.
But of Who was standing over it all.

I met Yeshua,
not the version the world shaped,
but the real *I AM*,
the Name above every name,
the radiance of YHWH's glory.

And that is when *yirah* was born in me.
Not because my life became easy.
Not because the battles ended.
But because the veil was lifted,
and I saw Him.

And once you have seen Him,
you can never unsee.
You can never go back
to the less of Him.

Everything simply connects,
align,
like missing pieces falling into place,
until the whole is revealed,
undeniable,
irrefutable,
mind-blowing.

# Chapter 24: Drawn Back to Propel Forward

Before the revelation,
I lived quiet and small.
Not because I feared speaking,
but because I felt everything so deeply.

As a highly sensitive soul,
rich in emotional intelligence and discernment
with an inner world that ran deep and vast,
I often chose stillness over noise,
silence over performance.

I've always believed in speaking up
for what is right.
But as I've grown
as He has refined me
my voice has grown bolder.
Fiercer.
Sharper for His glory.

Yeshua has been changing me
step by step,
softly,

steadily.

And one of the first changes I noticed
was my voice.

I no longer second-guess the urge to speak.
I no longer hold back when the fire is rising.

Instead, by His grace,
I speak
not to argue,
not to impress,
not to perform,
but to offer and reveal Him.

Words come now with greater calm.
With more clarity.
More weight.
Not born from self-confidence,
but from His strength flowing through my
yieldedness.

There is still so much more I hunger for:
more wisdom,
more eloquence,
more gentleness paired with boldness.

I don't desire these things to exalt myself.
I desire them to reflect Him rightly,
to stand in the places He calls me.
Unshaken by fear,
undistorted by insecurity.

I long to be a vessel
worthy of carrying His words.

And somewhere along this journey,
I began to see something deeper
about all the hardship,
all the tension,
all the waiting that had preceded this moment:

It was never wasted.

Like an arrow drawn back:
the further the tension,
the harder the pull,
the greater the future flight.

The hardship was the drawing.
The sadness the stretching.
The silence the pressure against the string.

And all along,

the hand of the Archer was steady.

In the waiting,
He received the glory.

And in the breakthrough,
He will receive it still.

I am the arrow.
He is the one who releases.

Not too soon.
Not too late.
But in the perfect fullness of His time.

# Chapter 25: The Key to Happiness
*And the Power of Being Still*

The key to happiness is not found in striving.
Not in forcing life to work on your own terms.
Not in holding onto past wounds
or future fears.

The key to happiness is surrender.

To surrender your whole life to Yeshua.
To surrender your past,
your present,
and your future into His hands.

To surrender all your pain,
all your sadness,
all your bitterness,
and to trust Him to deal with them.

You cannot carry these burdens alone.
You were never meant to.
You were never created to.

Only Yeshua can carry them.

Only Yeshua can heal what the world shattered.

He alone is strong enough to lift you.
Not by your might,
not by your striving,
but by His Spirit moving inside of you.

Happiness is not about pretending life
is perfect.
It's about handing your brokenness
to the only One who can redeem it.

It's about letting Him be
the Chief of your heart,
the Lord of your past,
the Keeper of your future.

It's about asking Him
to live so brightly within you
that when people look at your life,
they no longer simply see you—
they see Yeshua in you.

To YHWH be the glory, always.
(Ephesians 4:1-5, Philippians 2)

## Be Still and Know He Is God

Be still and know that He is God.
Not simply by waiting without movement
but by surrendering.

The Hebrew meaning of "be still" goes deeper
than quietness.
It means:
to surrender,
to release,
to let go,
to become weak,
so that you can truly know He is in control.

To be still is not to be abandoned.
It is to stop clinging to your own strength,
and to rest in the everlasting arms of the I AM.

It is to release the battles you cannot win on
your own,
the wounds you cannot heal by yourself,
the future you cannot control.

It is to trust
that He is still God,

even when you are still,
even when you are weak,
even when all you can do is surrender.

Because the I AM does not leave those
who lean on Him.

And only then will you truly know—

*He is* **YHWH Yeshua**.

יהוה

# Chapter 26: I Am Sahar: Dawn

My name is Sahar,
*Shachar* in Hebrew which means *dawn*.

The first light that breaks through the darkness.
It is not loud,
but it is dramatic.
It does not demand attention,
but it cannot be ignored.

Dawn is where everything begins again.
Where night ends
and newness is born.
Where the world crosses quietly
into another chance at life.

The dawn am not the midday sun.
It is the signal that it's coming.

And just like dawn,
I rise not to be seen
but to say,
*"This is the time.
Something new is being born."*

At the time of writing this,
I find myself standing at a crossing point,
one that, without my planning,
happens to align with a number
rich in meaning throughout Scripture.

A number that has always marked the end
of wilderness,
the beginning of purpose,
and the birth of new seasons.

I didn't orchestrate this.
But somehow,
the timing and the symbolism found me
just as I was ready to step forward.

And so,
I do not take this transition lightly.

I lay it down.
I lift it up.
I offer it to the One who shaped me
with mercy in His breath
and purpose in His hands.

I will not step into this season seeking
applause..
I will not gather those who already have
enough.

Instead,

I will prepare a banquet
for the poor,
the hungry,
the humble.

Like the parable Yeshua gave,
I will say:
I do not want a party.
I want to build an altar.
A place where sacrifice becomes worship,
and obedience becomes breakthrough.

This is my transition.
This is my crossing over.
This is the season where old stories end,
and the I AM writes a new one.

And I declare this not for applause
but for alignment.

I am Sahar.
And Sahar means *dawn—shachar*.
Through Him, He births newness
not with noise,
but with light.
Not in pride,
but in purpose.

Let the darkness flee.
Let the hungry be fed.
Let the future unfold.
Let the Kingdom come.

To **Yeshua** be the glory.

*Yeshua means YHWH is salvation—
the God who saves*

# Chapter 27: To the One Who Stayed Until the End

Perhaps you did laugh once
but now, you weep.

Perhaps you did shrug
but now, you tremble.

Perhaps you did mock
but now, you sit in silence.

That means something.
That means you heard something.

This is not a religion.
Forget religion.

This is a call to return to the Root:
The only Root.
The One from whom all things came,
and to whom all things will return.

You can walk away.
You're free to chant the mantra:
"Better to die and find out there is no God,

than to believe
and find out too late that there was."

But this is your burden of proof now.
The onus is on you.
My hands are washed clean.

I wrote what I was told to write.
I said what I had to say.
I burned so that you could see the fire.
I shattered so you could hear the cry.

So here you are.
And here He is.
Not a myth.
Not a crutch.
Not a metaphor.

The I AM.
Yeshua.
Yahweh.
One and the Same.

This is the only Truth that will matter
the moment your *breath* leaves your body.
You stayed until the end.
That was no accident.

Now it's your turn
to answer Him.

## Epilogue: The Last Cry Before the Break

This is not the end.
This is the thunder before the sky splits.
This is the voice crying out,
"Prepare the way of YHWH."

I did not write this to win affection.
Though I am human enough to long for it.
If applause were my aim,
I would not have undressed my soul like this.
I would not have laid my wounds bare—
open to be mocked, misunderstood,
or dismissed.

I did not bleed these pages to be understood.
I did not cry these laments to fit inside your bookshelf.
I cried them because the time is short
and the veil is lifting.

Yeshua is not coming back quietly.

He will not return as a whisper.
He will return as the Consuming Fire.

He will return as the Judge.
He will return as the I AM
who was never absent,
only withheld.

This was never just a book.
This was an altar.
Each word a stone.
Each cry a matchstick.
And now, the fire is lit.

To the world that mocked Him:
You will see Him.

To the ones who forgot Him:
You will remember.

To the ones who never knew Him:
You will bow
by choice
or by tremble.

For every tear I have cried,
every ache I have written,
every fury I have groaned in the dark—

He heard it.

And He is coming.

This is your last cry before the break.
This is your final whisper before the trumpet.
This is the time of reckoning.

The time of revealing.
The time of the remnant rising.

You were not meant to blend in.
You were not meant to bow to man.
You were not meant to flirt with darkness
and then cry when it swallows you.

You were made for light.
You were made to know Him.
You were made to stand in fire
and not be burned.

So I say this,
not in fear,
but in authority,
because the One who gave me this voice
also gave me the fire.

Yeshua is YHWH.
Not a god among the many.

Not a name you toss into your prayers.

He is **YHWH Elohim,**
**the only Elohim.**

He is the Name above all names.
The Breath in your lungs.
The Truth the world cannot dilute.
The Fire the darkness cannot quench.

The **Ancient of Days**
far above your extraterrestrials,
Annunakis,
and every other fallen or created host
operating under corrupted authority —
once granted,
now defiled.

So choose.
Not later.
Not someday.
Now.

Choose whom you will serve.
For you can only have one Master,
one Father:

either the created,
or the **Uncreated One.**

Either the counterfeit,
or the **Only Original.**

Either the limited,
or the **Absolute.**

There is no middle ground.
Descend without Him
into the judgment of fire.

Or ascend with Him
into the glory of salvation.

Because this was your warning.
This was your invitation.
And this…

Was your *dawn*.

For behold —

the *Light* has come.

# Postlude: The Dawn. A Meditation

The dawn is a loud whisper,
barely heard, yet impossible to ignore.

It does not shout.
It speaks in stillness,
like wind brushing through the trees
gentle, but undeniable.

It moves without fanfare,
arriving not in blinding flash,
but in a slow unfolding of light.

Soft enough to go unnoticed,
yet bright enough to banish shadows.

It does not demand to be seen.
It cannot be unseen.

The dawn stirs what has been sleeping.
Not with force,
but with quiet authority.

It reminds the world that morning has come

and that something new is beginning.

It changes everything
simply by rising.

And so did I
by His grace alone.

I am here not because the road was smooth.
I am here because I did not stop walking.
I did not stop writing.
I did not stop believing
even when the night was long,
even when no one was watching.

This book was not born of ease,
but of endurance,
and surrender to Him.

It is proof that light still rises
when the soul refuses to quit.

It is steady.
It is certain.
It is gentle,
relentless,
and it is unstoppable.

This is the mystery of the dawn:
not in its volume,
but in its presence.

The *dawn* is the first light
that breaks through the darkness.

It is not loud
but it is dramatic.
It does not demand attention,
but it cannot be ignored.

Dawn is the beginning of new mercies.
Where night ends and newness is born.
Where the world crosses quietly
into another chance at life.

The dawn rises to be seen,
to signal His coming,
the unveiling of a Greater Dawn,
deliverance at hand.

For the last trump will sound,
the asleep will awake,
caught up with the sealed ones.

It is the dawn of a Great Day
A day the world has not yet seen.

**He** is *near*.

# Author's Final Note

If you found yourself in these pages,
I want you to know
you were never alone.

I wrote this because I lived it.
And I wrote it so that someone like you
would finally see the fire in their own bones.

That even dry bones can rise.
Even silence can speak.
Even graves can echo with glory,
if He wills it,
and if you believe.

Because it's never been about being worthy.
It's always been about surrender.

And if your spirit is still trembling,
then maybe, just maybe,

*the resurrection*
   *has already begun*
      *in you.*

# Acknowledgments

To the One who allowed me to cry,
to vex,
to question,
to wonder,
to desire,
and even to fall.

You let me choose,
not because You are distant,
but because You are love.

And through every ache,
You waited
not with wrath,
but with arms ready to embrace.

To the One who gave me breath
who alone can extinguish it,
or breathe it again into dry bones,
even when I've become nothing but ashes.

You allowed me to experience *yirah*:
holy, trembling awe.

And there are no words strong enough
to describe how wonderful You are.

Thank You for choosing someone like me:
a broken vessel,
a sinner once stained scarlet,
now made white only by You.

Thank You for calling me.
Thank You for shielding me.
Thank You for letting me glorify You
with what little I have.

I am nothing without You.
But You,
You are worthy of all.

So I give this book,
this offering,
this journey
back to You.

      Glory be to my **Melech haOlam,**

          **YHWH Yeshua.**

# About the Author

Sahar Soltani is a voice forged in fire,
a woman who has walked through the
wilderness, wrestled in the silence,
and risen with a pen soaked in both pain and
power. She writes not for applause,
but for awakening.

Her words are for the ones who feel too much,
for the misfits,
the tender-hearted,
the seers,
the ones who almost gave up
but didn't.

Her calling is not to entertain
but to unveil:
truth,
holiness,
and the Name above every name.

A survivor of betrayal,
loneliness,
loss,

and years of spiritual anguish,
Sahar now stands as a vessel
marked by the Fire.
Her prophetic writing is a cry from the depths:
a lament turned to declaration,
a scroll for the remnant.

She is the author of:
**Unmasking the Trinity: Yeshua is Yahweh**
*The Oneness That Was Hidden All Along,*
**You Don't Fit In:** *Because the Surface World Cannot Handle Discerning Minds*
**The Dogs Are Boiled Alive While the World Pretends To Care**

She writes for those who still feel the ache of Eden, who burn for truth,
and who long to know the I AM for themselves.

Her life is not a brand.
It is a broken altar,
a place of surrender,
rebuilt by mercy.

Many of the writings in this book were drawn directly from her lifelong journals,
pages poured out in solitude,

through tears,
anguish,
fury,
fire,
and whispered cries
when she no longer wanted to live.

This was not curated.
It was carved from the rawest places of the soul
written with her spirit laid bare,
as a testament that she lives
because of Him.

## To YHWH Yeshua be the glory.

# Other Works by the Author

**You Don't Fit In:** *Because the Surface World Cannot Handle Discerning Minds*
The original version of this book, a raw, poetic manifesto for the misfits, the visionaries, and those the world often misunderstands and labels "too much."

It speaks to those who feel deeply, think critically, and refuse to conform to shallow expectations.
But it's also written for those on the other side, those who may not have felt this way but are ready to understand and honour those who do. Because respecting what is rare is just as important as protecting it.

**You Don't Fit In (Children's Edition)**
A beautifully adapted version for children ages 8–12 who feel different, sensitive, or out of place.
This edition helps young minds understand that their depth is not a flaw but a strength.

**Unmasking the Trinity Yeshua is YHWH:** *The Oneness That Was Hidden All Along.*
A piercing restoration and declaration that Yeshua is not a separate figure, but YHWH Himself revealed. Written for those who have wrestled with distorted doctrines and longed to return to the unfiltered truth.

**The Undefiled One:** *The Ancient of Days Who Trampled Decay*
A cry of awe and testimony to Yeshua's incorruptible nature, This work unveils His purity, His identity as YHWH, and His victory over every form of decay.

**The Restoration of 4 Ezra (2 Esdras) Recovered for the Remnant:** *A Faithful Reconstruction of YHWH's Word Based on Surviving Manuscripts*
A restored translation of the apocalyptic text once removed from canon, carrying visions of judgment, hope, and the hidden books reserved for the end times.

**The Dogs Are Boiled Alive While the World Pretends to Care:** *A Cry for the Dogs of Yulin and for the Silence That Keeps Them Burning.*
A heartbreaking exposé of the Yulin Dog Meat Festival and the world's silence toward animal cruelty.
This is both a cry for justice and a call to conscience. Written for those who can no longer look away.

To read more, follow, or connect with the author:
Email: quietseerpress@outlook.com
saharsoltani.author@outlook.com

# Final Scripture Seal
*Let the Truth Be the Last Word*

*Yeshua said to them,*
*Amen, amen, I say to you,*
*before Abraham came to be, **I AM**.*
– John 8:58

*Yeshua said, When you lift up the Son of Man,*
*then you shall know that **I AM**,*
*and that I do none at all of Myself,*
*but as My Father taught Me,*
*these words I speak.*
– John 8:28

*I and the Father are One.*
– John 10:30

*I am the Alpha and the Omega,*
*the Beginning and the End,*
*says **YHWH**, the One who is, and who was,*
*and who is to come, the Almighty.*
– Revelation 1:8

*And when I saw Him,*
*I fell at His feet as dead.*
*But He placed His right hand on me, saying,*
*Do not fear, I am the First and the Last,*
*and the Living One.*
*And I became dead,*
*and see, I am alive forever and ever.*
*And I possess the keys of She'ol and of Death.*
– Revelation 1:17–18


*Everyone who calls on the Name of* **YHWH**
*shall be saved.*
– Joel 2:32


*Therefore I said to you that*
*you shall die in your sins,*
*for unless you believe*
*that* **I AM***,*
*you shall die in your sins.*
– John 8:24


And His Name is **Yeshua***.*
He is **YHWH***.*
He is the **I AM***.*

# Notes

# Notes

# Notes

www.ingramcontent.com/pod-product-compliance
Lightning Source LLC
Chambersburg PA
CBHW020340010526
44119CB00048B/546